MW00699777

2600 Typographic Ornaments & Designs

selected and arranged by

Maggie Kate

DOVER PUBLICATIONS, INC.
Mineola, New York

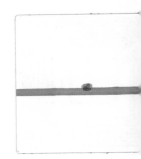

Copyright

Copyright © 2001 by Dover Publications, Inc.
All rights reserved under Pan American and International Copyright Conventions.

Bibliographical Note

2600 Typographic Ornaments and Designs, first published in 2001, is a compilation of most of the material from *Allerlei Zierat: Zur Ausstattung Von Drucksachen Jeden Charakters,* originally published in Leipzig, c. 1902, by J. G. Schelter & Giesecke. The contents have been selected and arranged by Maggie Kate. And an introductory Note has been specially prepared for this edition.

DOVER *Pictorial Archive* SERIES

This book belongs to the Dover Pictorial Archive Series. You may use the designs and illustrations for graphics and crafts applications, free and without special permission, provided that you include no more than ten in the same publication or project. (For permission for additional use, please write to Permissions Department, Dover Publications, Inc., 31 East 2nd Street, Mineola, N.Y. 11501.)

However, republication or reproduction of any illustration by any other graphic service, whether it be in a book or in any other design resource, is strictly prohibited.

Library of Congress Cataloging-in-Publication Data

Kate, Maggie.
    2600 typographic ornaments and designs / selected and arranged by Maggie Kate.
        p. cm. — (Dover pictorial archive series)
    "A compilation of most of the material from Allerlei Zierat: zur Ausstattung von Drucksachen jeden Charakters, originally published in Leipzig, c. 1902 by J. G. Schelter & Giesecke."
    ISBN 0-486-41798-0
    1. Type ornaments—Specimens. 2. Printers' ornaments—Specimens. 3. J. G. Schelter & Giesecke. 4. Type and type-founding—Germany—Liepzig—History. I. Title: Two thousand six hundred typographic ornaments and designs. II. J. G. Schelter & Giesecke. Allerlei Zierat: zur Ausstattung von Drucksachen jeden Charakters. III. Title. IV. Series.

Z250.3 .K38 2001
686.2'24—dc21

                                       2001032351

Manufactured in the United States of America
Dover Publications, Inc., 31 East 2nd Street, Mineola, N.Y. 11501

NOTE

This richly diverse compendium of typographical ornaments is culled from a turn-of-the-century catalog of the German foundry established in 1819 in Leipzig by punchcutter Johann Schelter and typefounder Christian Giesecke. Catalogs such as theirs were made possible by the invention of electrotype around 1850, and they offered for sale to printing jobbers a tremendous assortment of printer's ornaments, as well as cast type in various faces. The cost of each ornament varied from fifteen cents to three dollars, depending on size. Ever since the invention of the printing press in the fifteenth century, printers have used decorative ornaments to fill space in page layouts and enliven the printed page. These designs can be distinguished from illustrations in that they have no connection with the content of the text, being purely decorative.

Many of the items contained herein show the influence of the Art Nouveau movement in the applied and decorative arts that flourished on the continent around the same time this catalog was published. In Germany, "Art Nouveau" (new art) was known as "Jugendstil"—or youth style—after the magazine *Jugend* (youth). The style was characterized by dominant undulating lines or contours to which all other elements (like color, form, and texture) were secondary, and it was greeted as a new and revitalizing force in the arts. The origins of the movement are manifold, encompassing a broad spectrum of influences including William Morris' Arts and Crafts movement of the 1870s, which sought to grant crafts the same status as that accorded to painting and sculpture. In turn, this movement—which so highly valued the expression of individuality inherent in handicrafts—was at least in part a reaction against the new machine age of mass production heralded by the Industrial Revolution.

This volume has been assembled with the idea in mind of maximum usability for contemporary artists and craftspeople. The ornaments and designs make an attractive complement to typography in all types of printed material, including books, letterheads, newsletters, and package design. They also may be used anywhere that small and elegant designs are required—in needlework and leathercraft, for example.

3

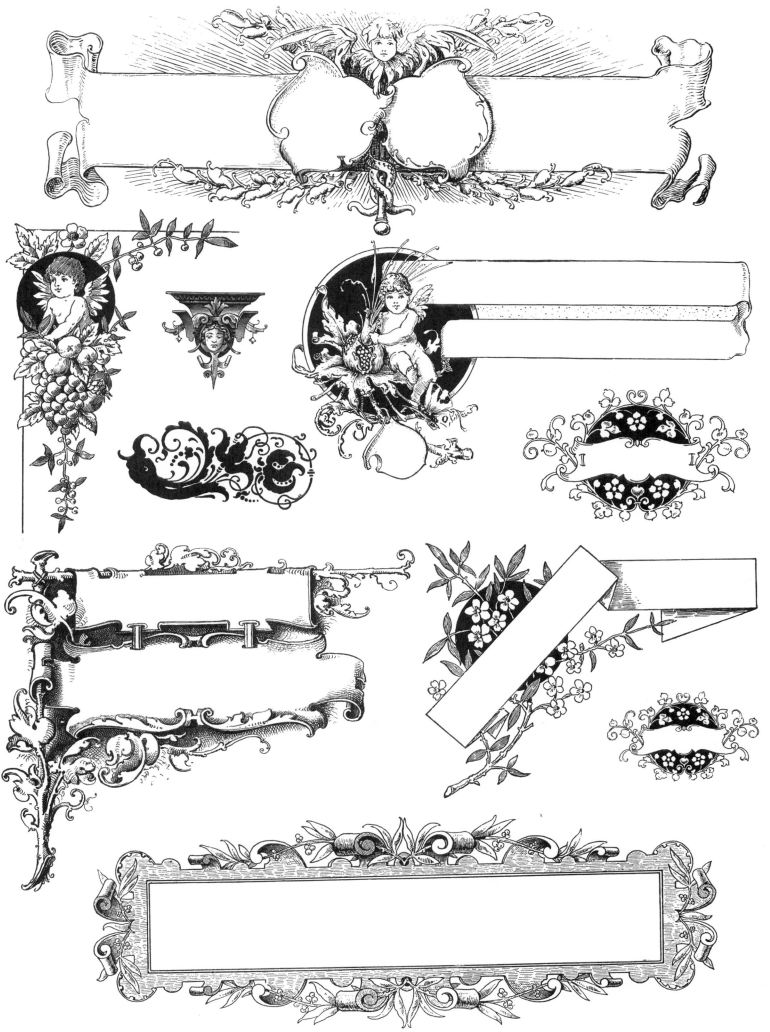

7

8

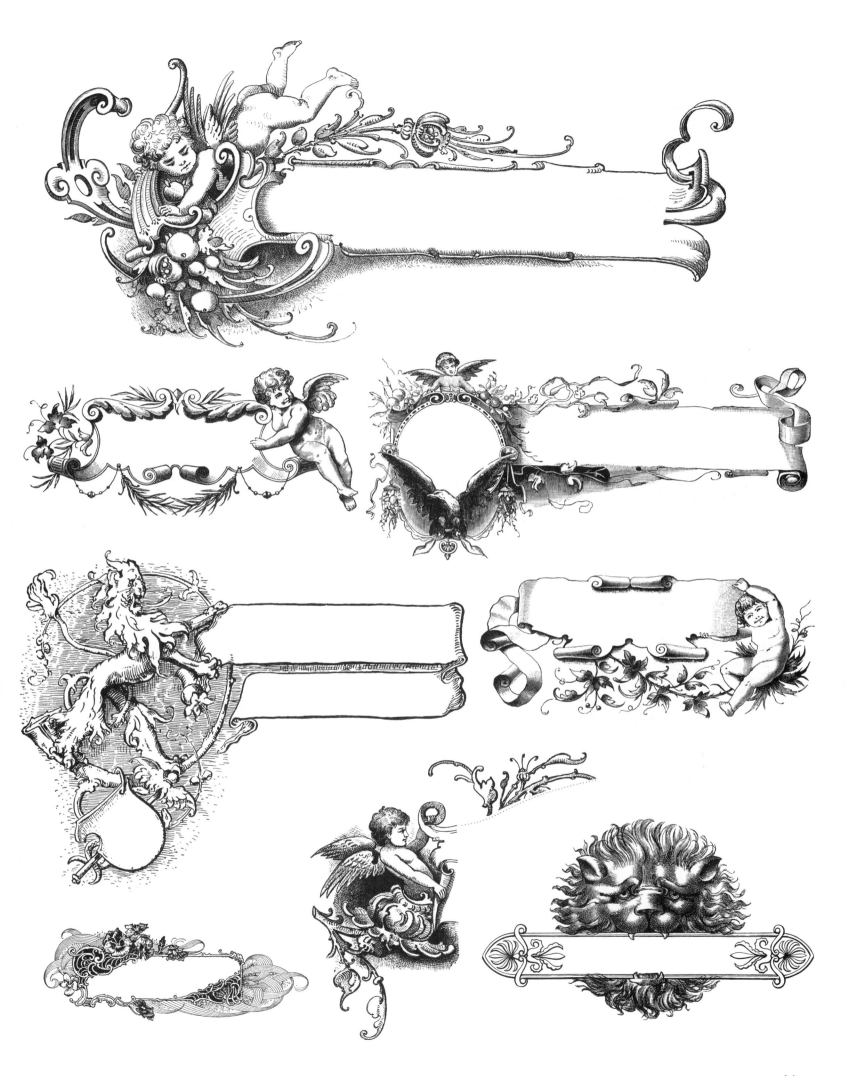

13

19

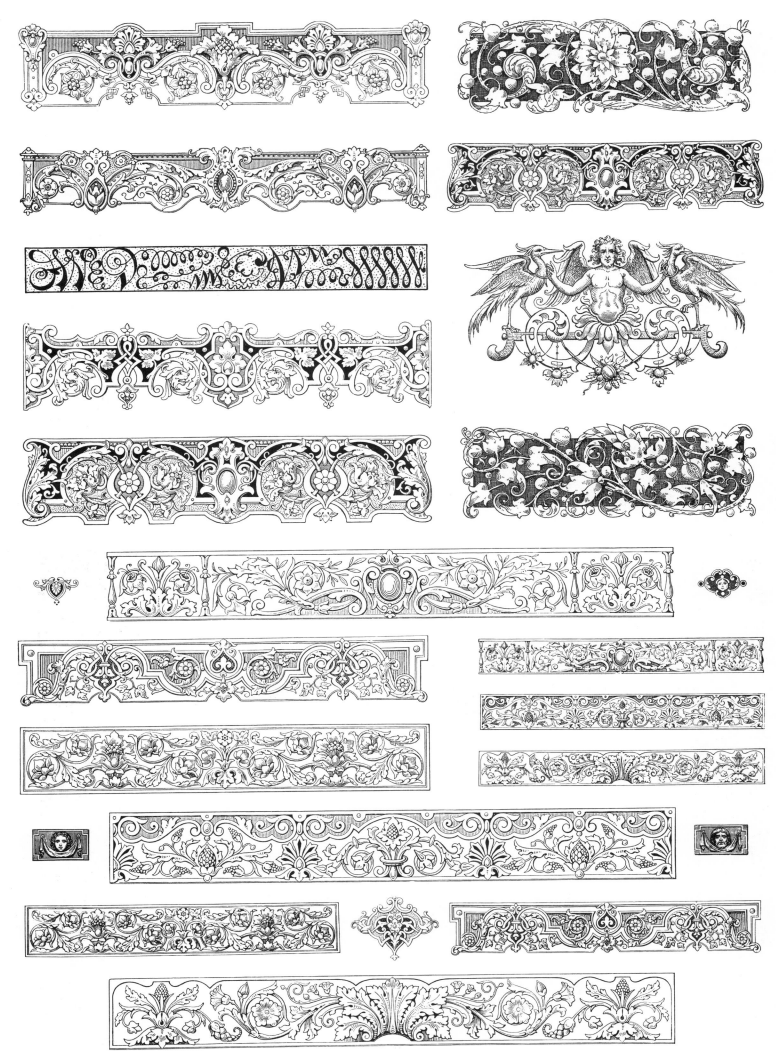

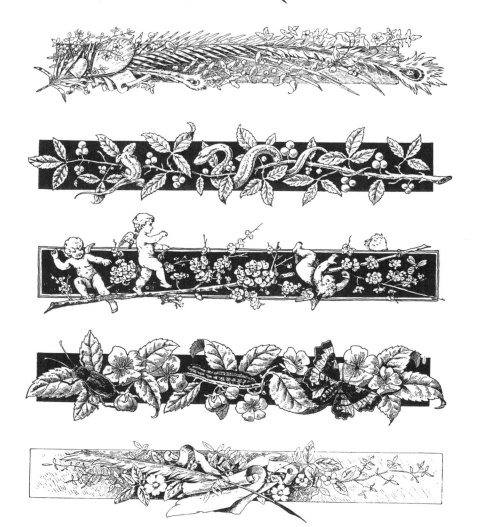

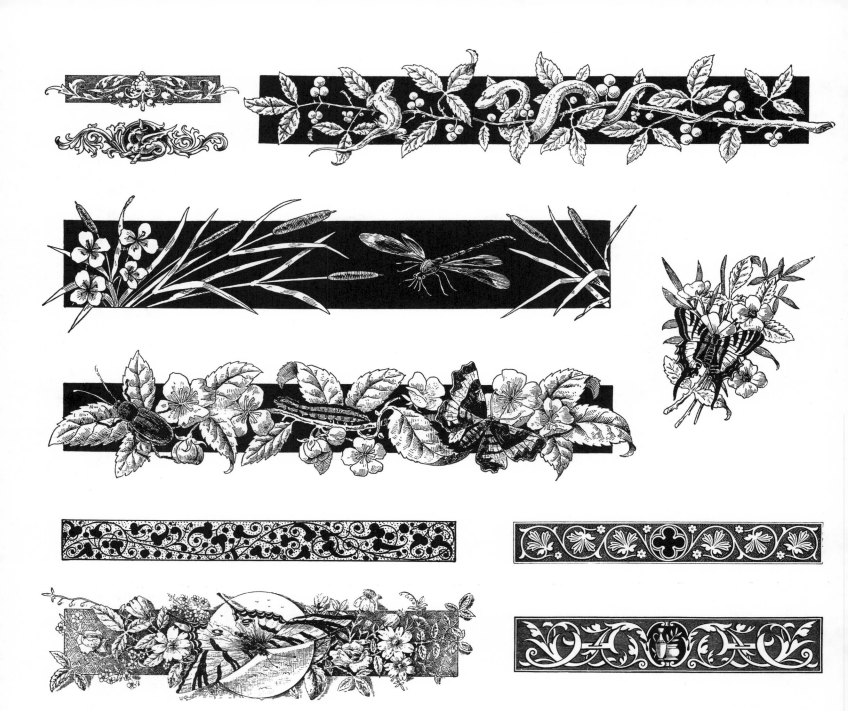

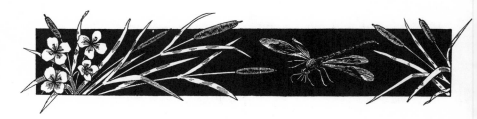

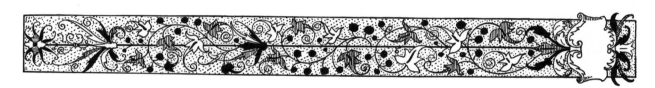

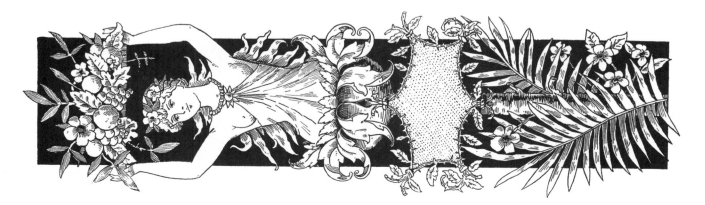

31

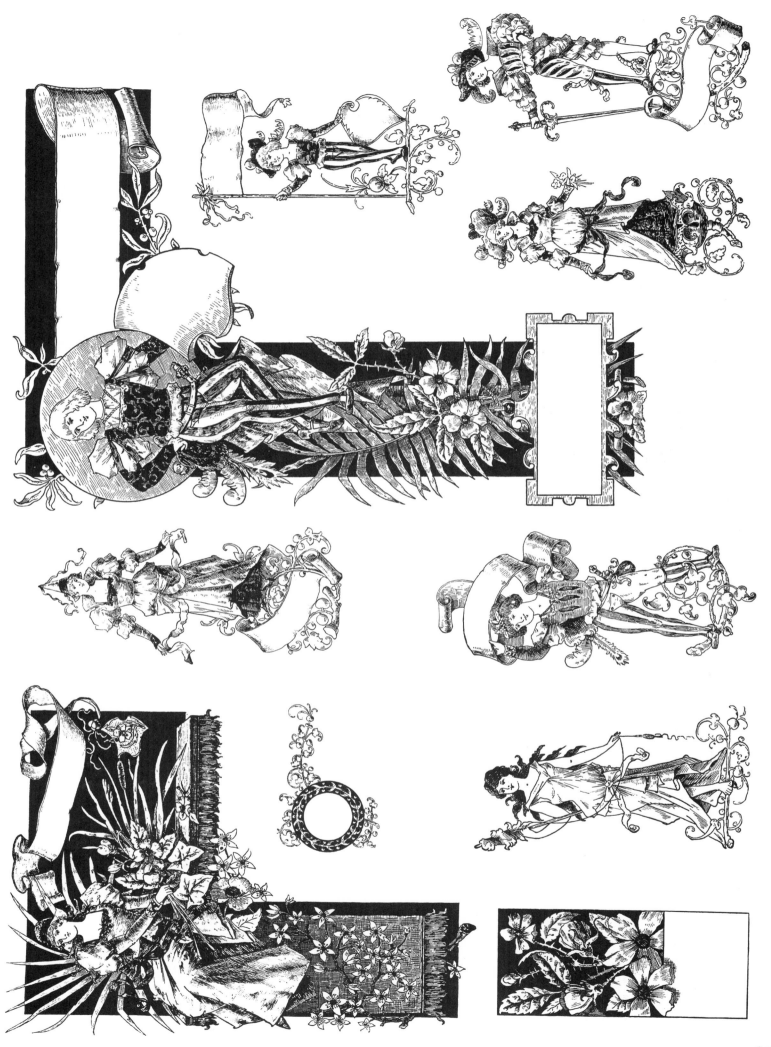

36

41

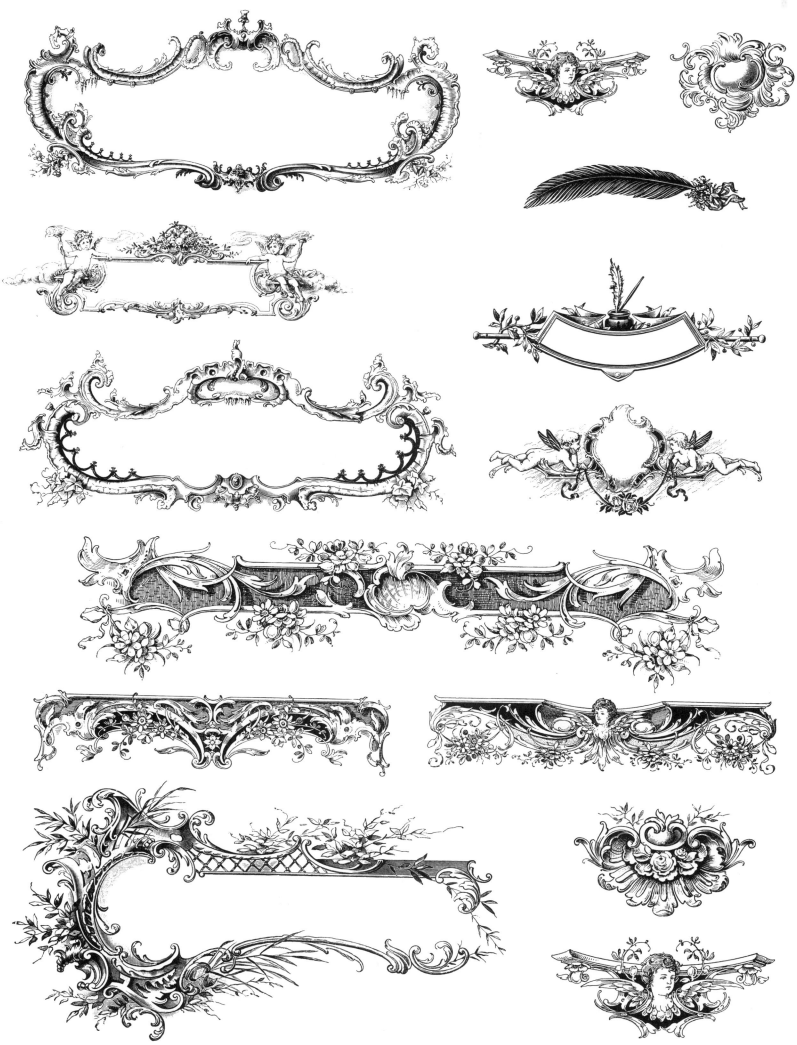

44

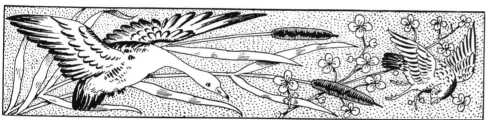

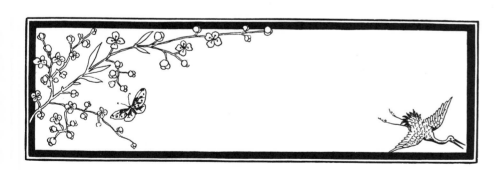

45

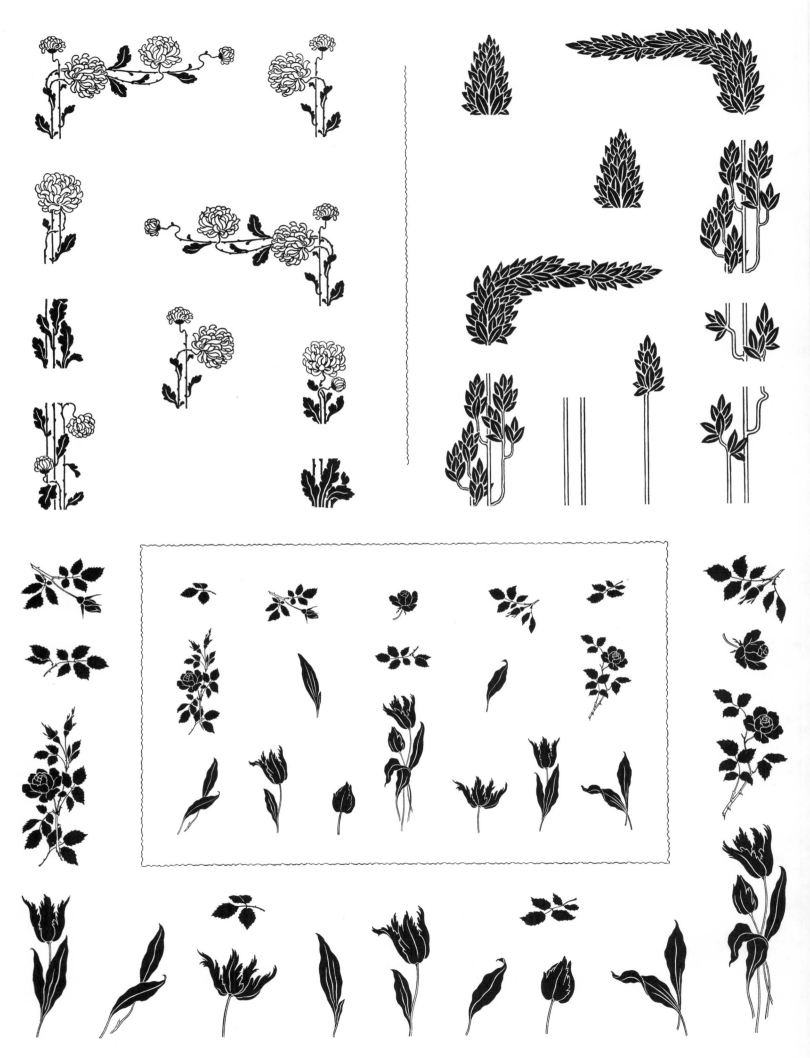

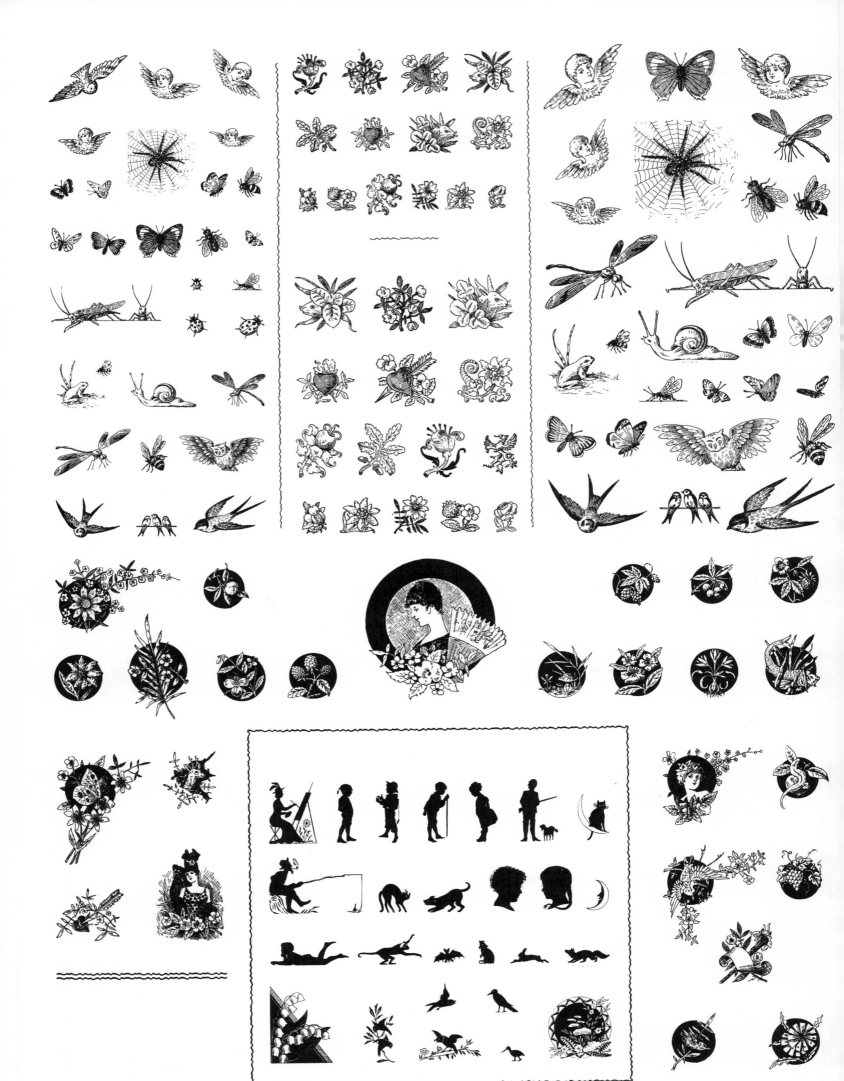

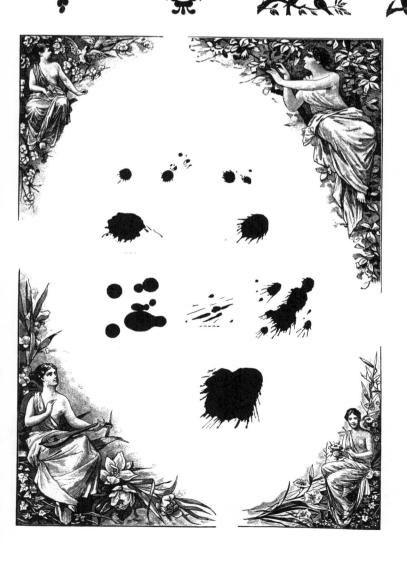

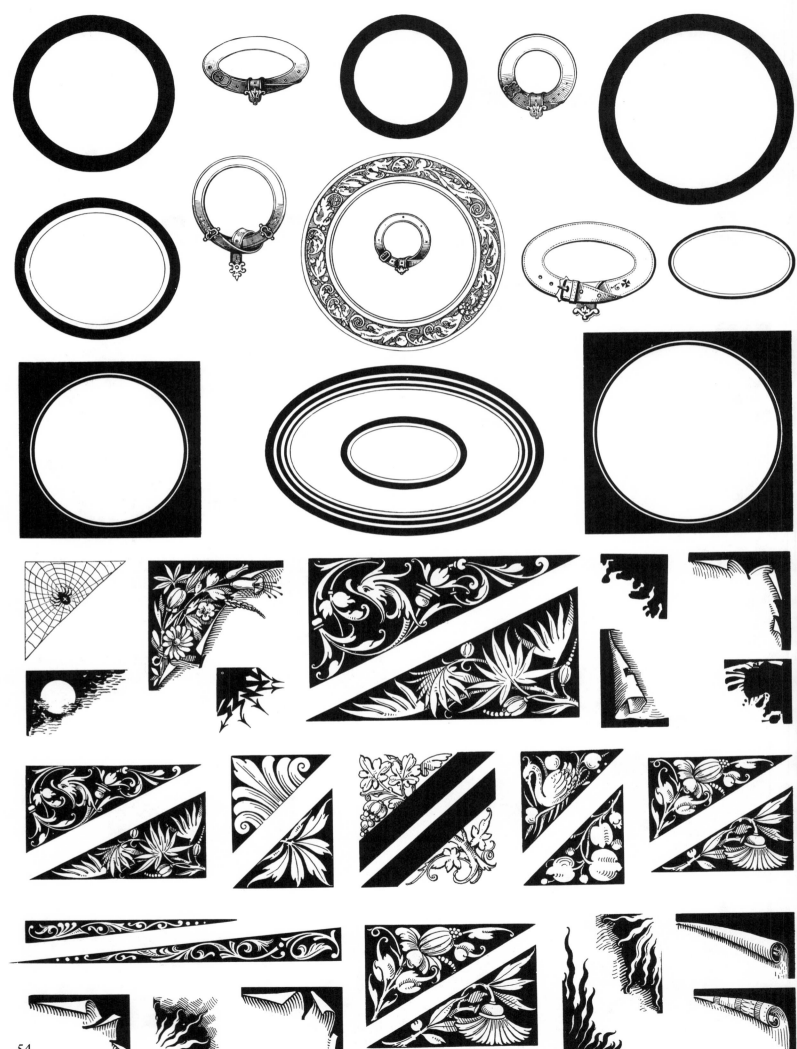

57

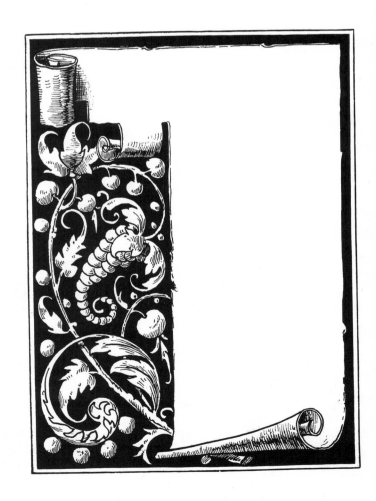

60

61

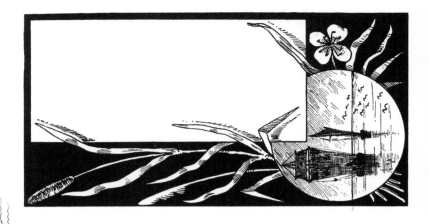

67

69

MENU

70

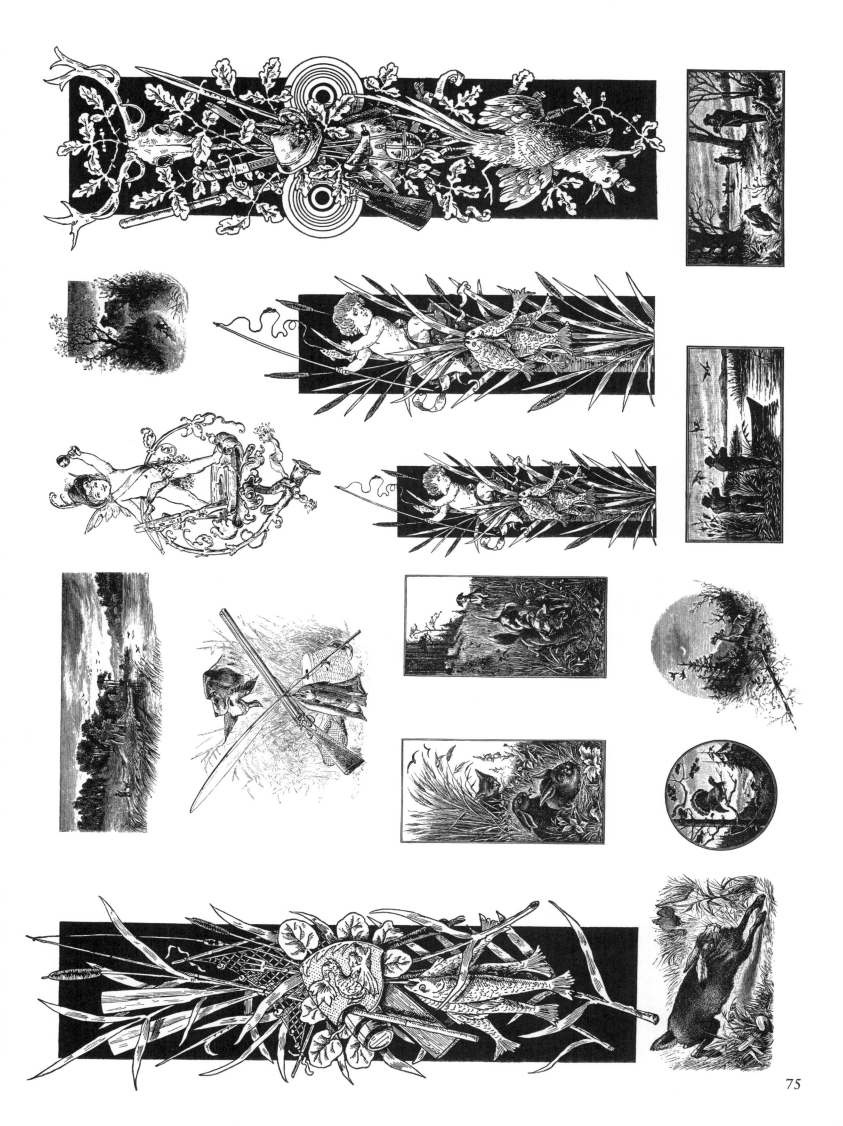

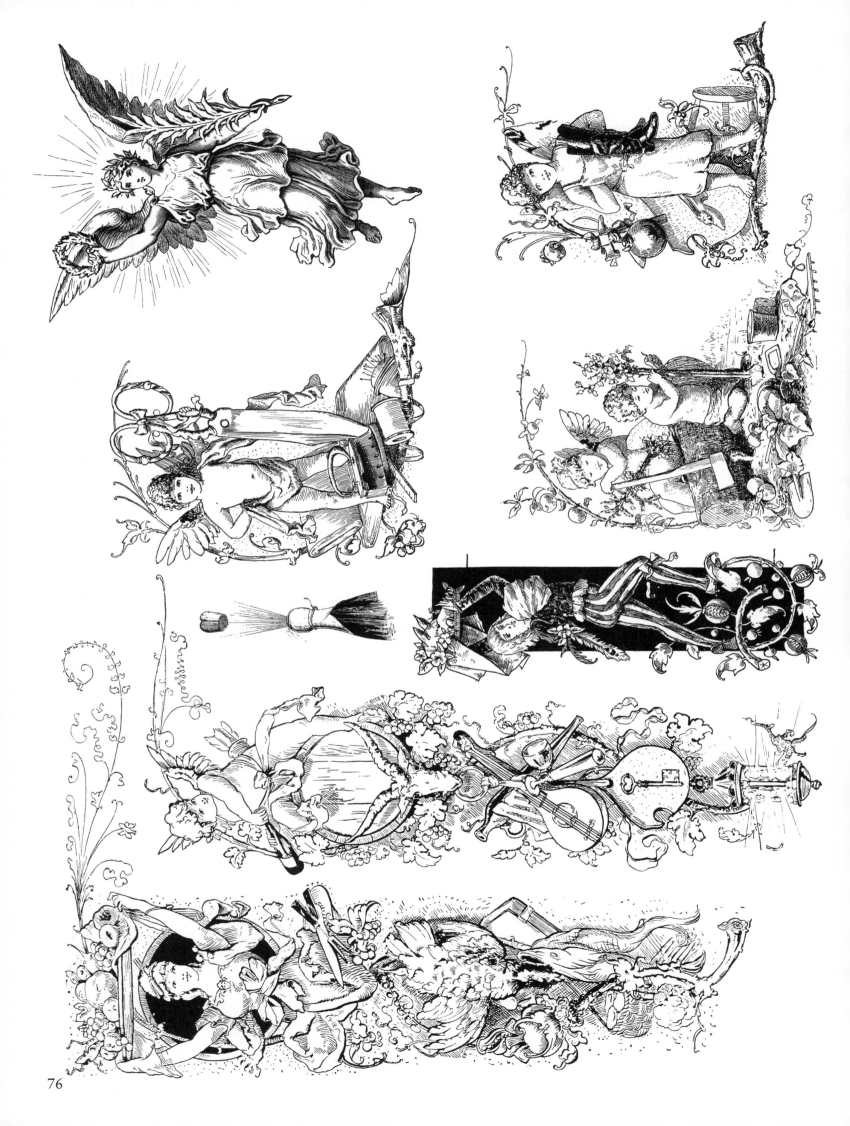

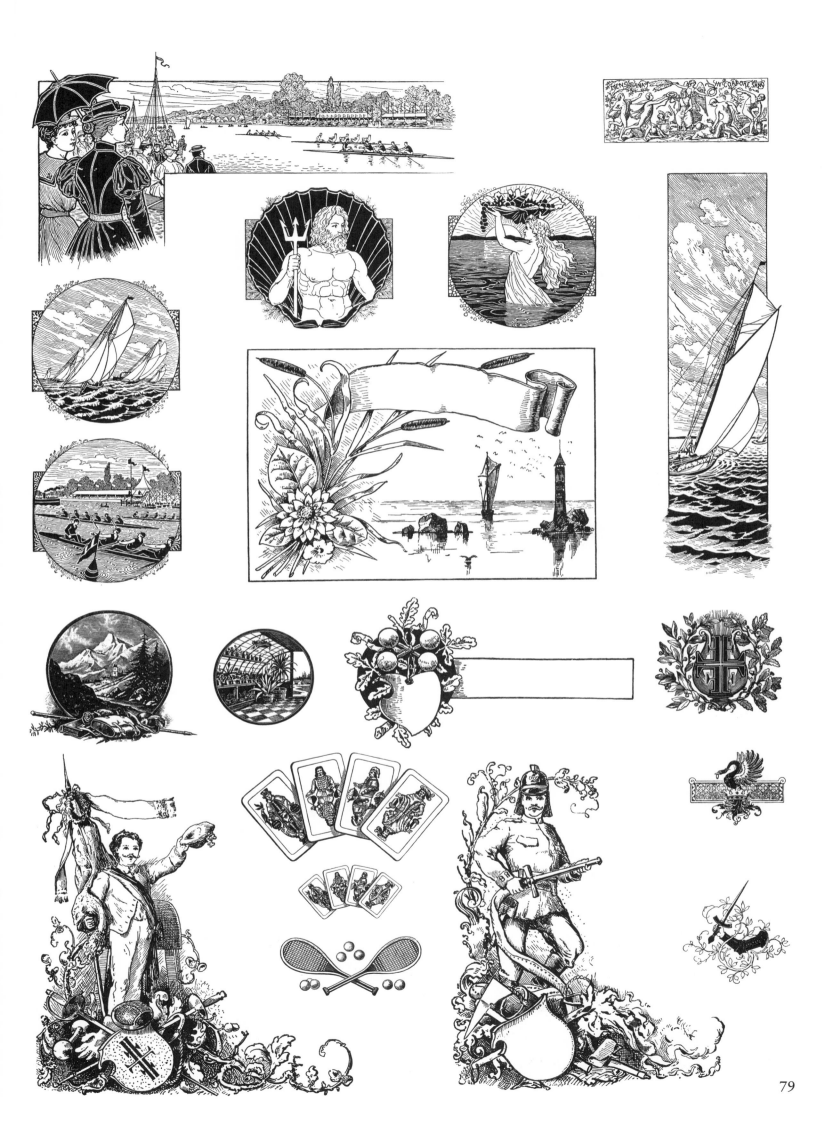

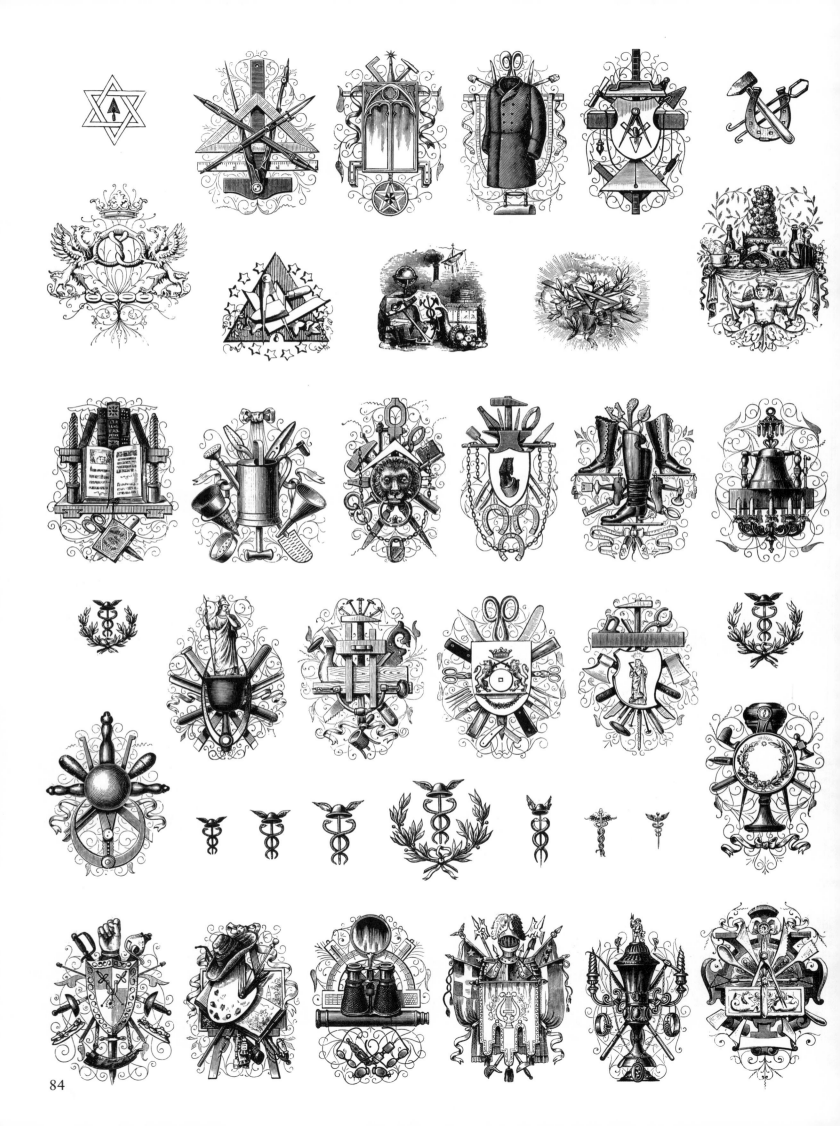

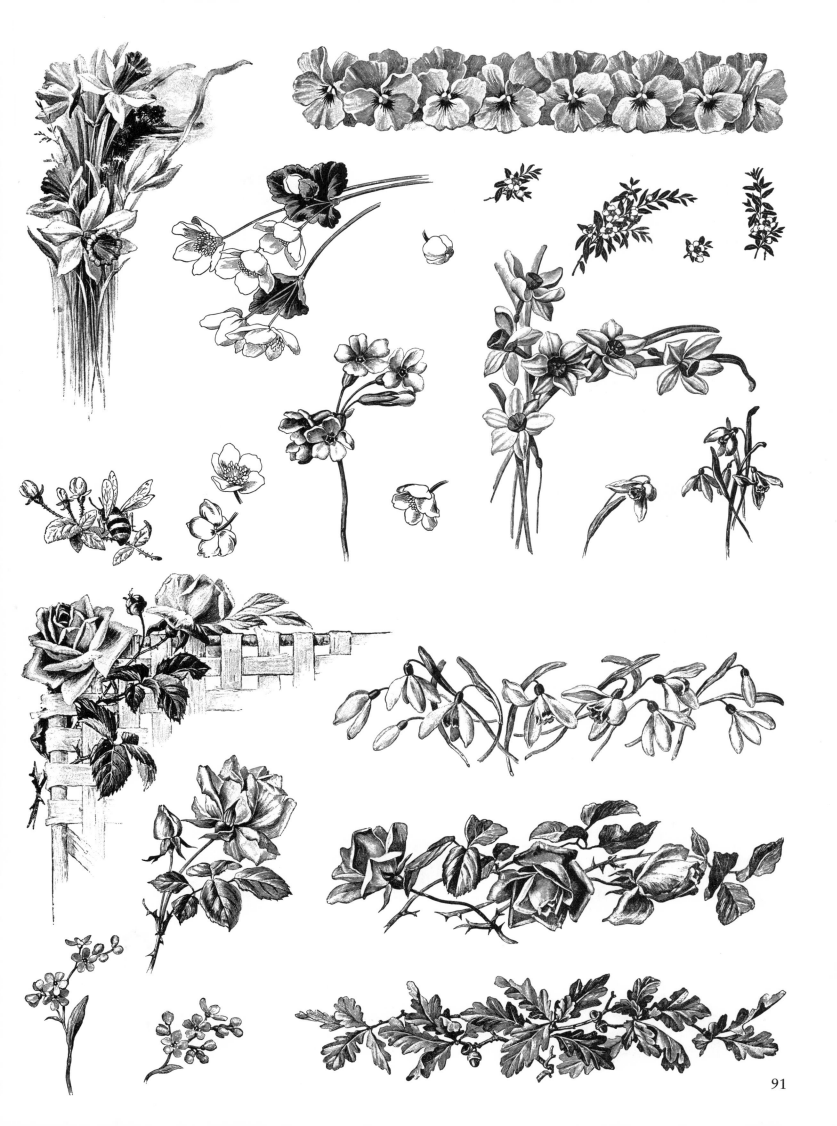

91

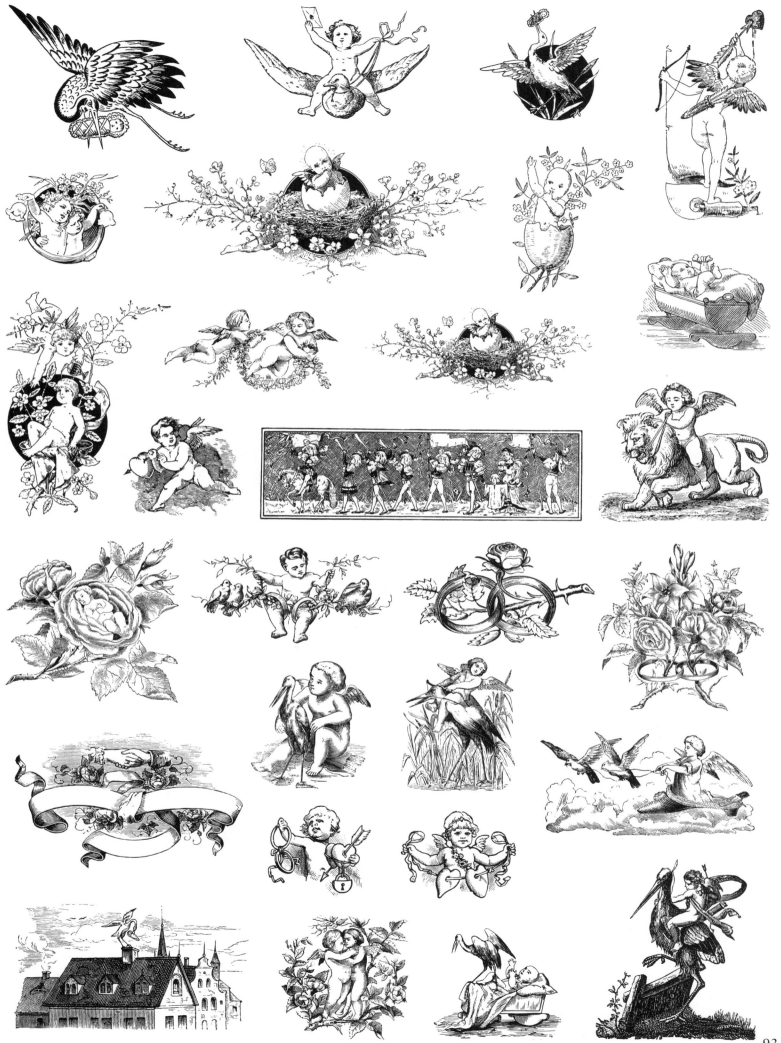

95

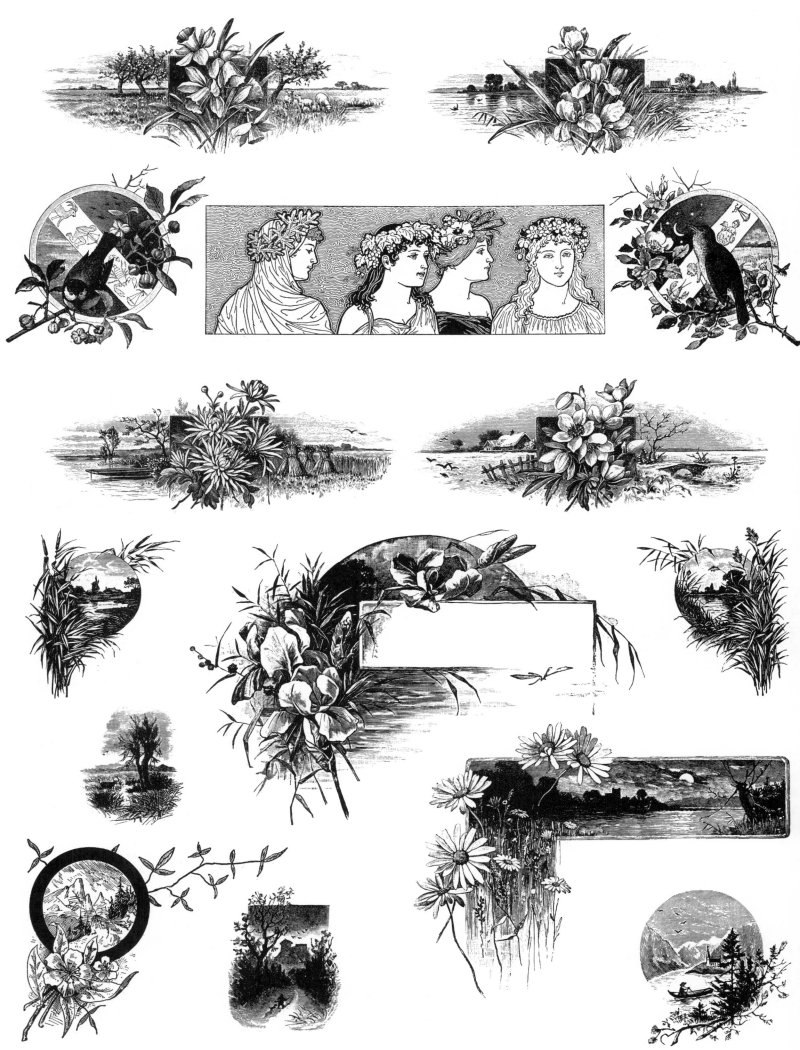

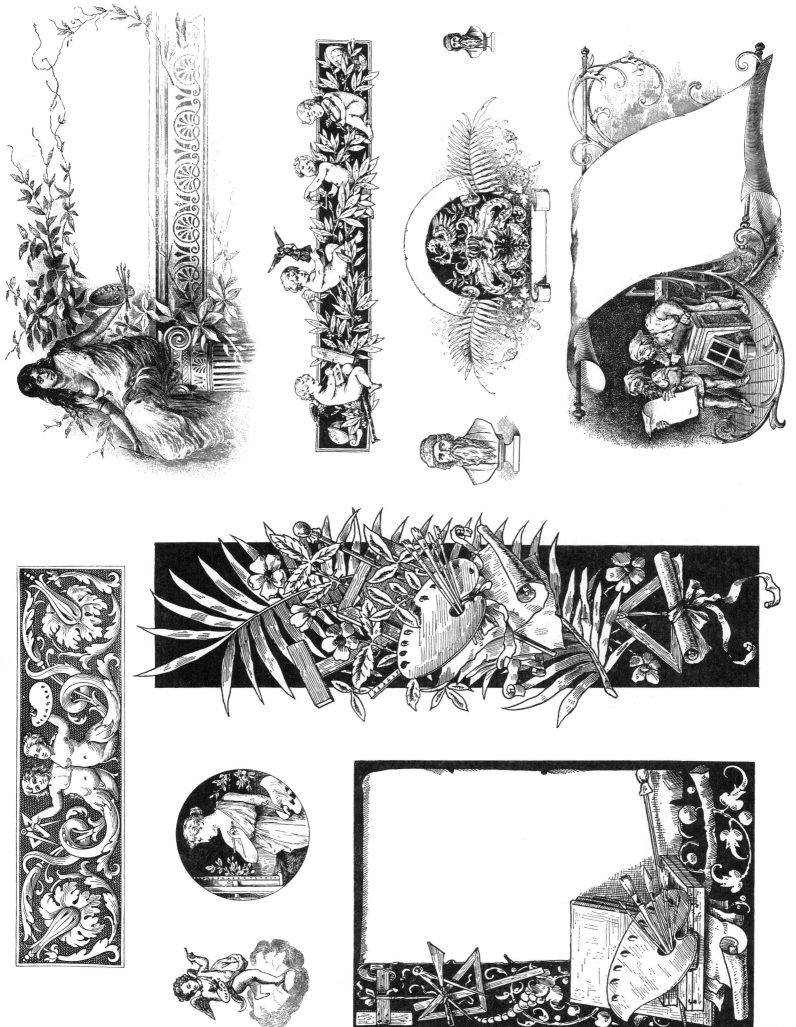

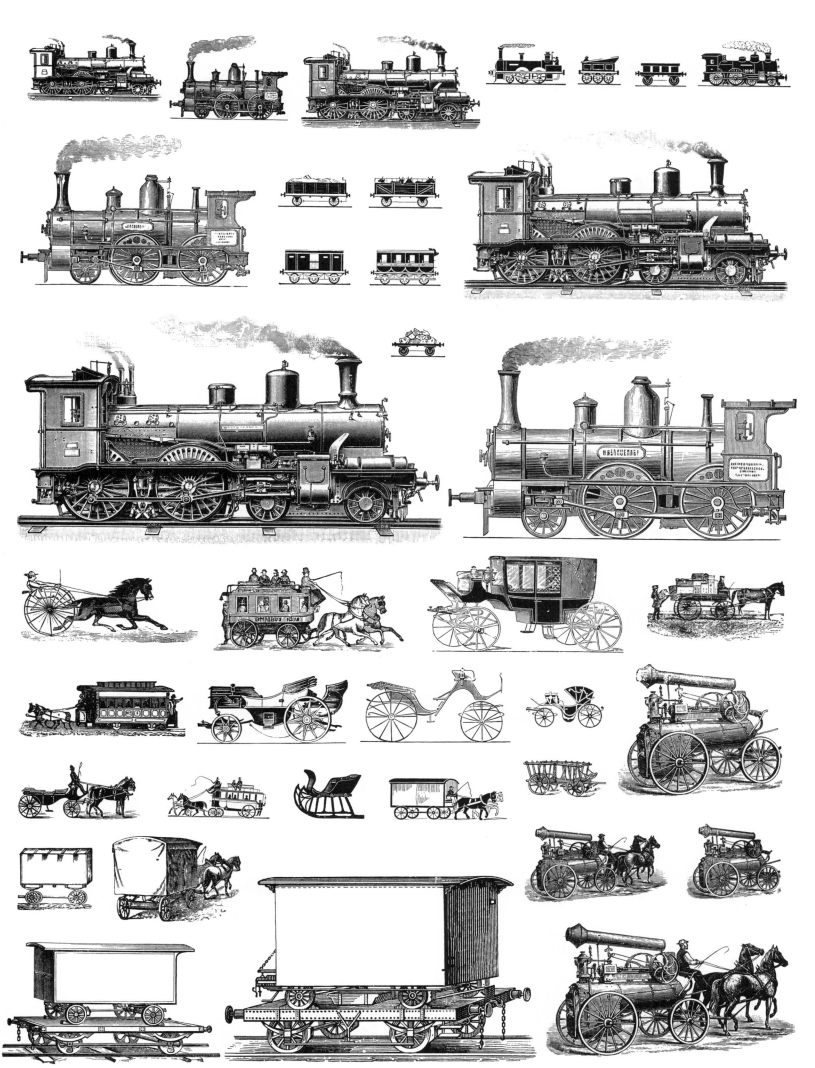

112

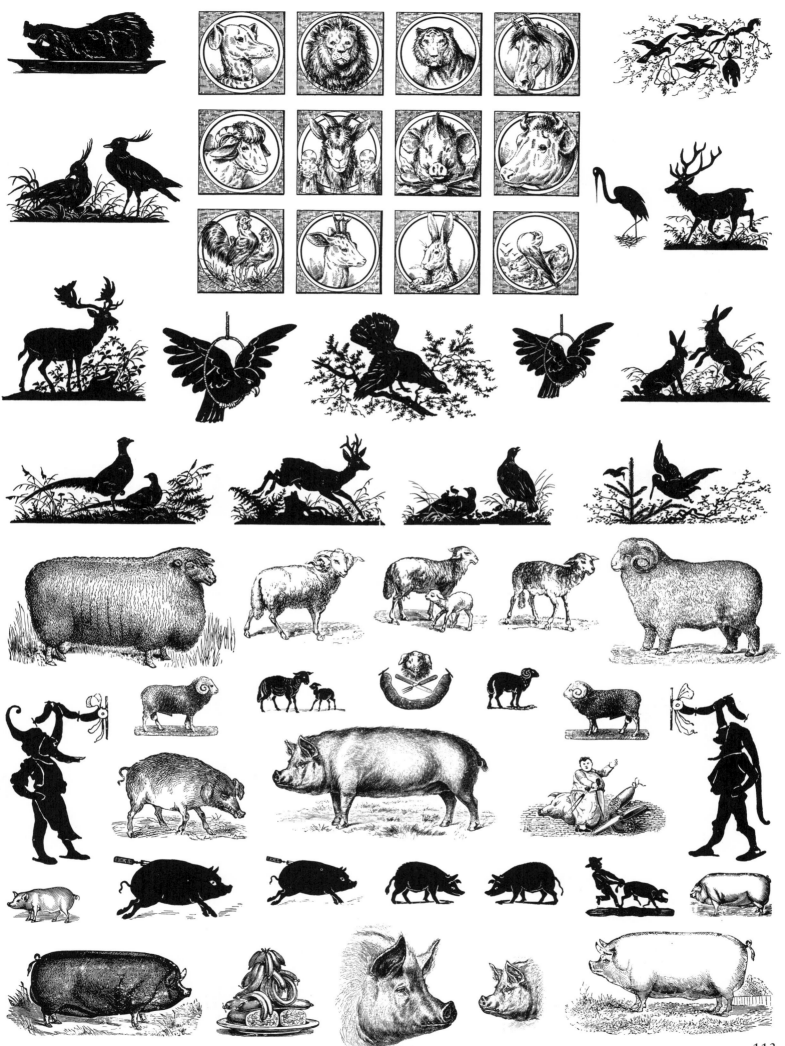

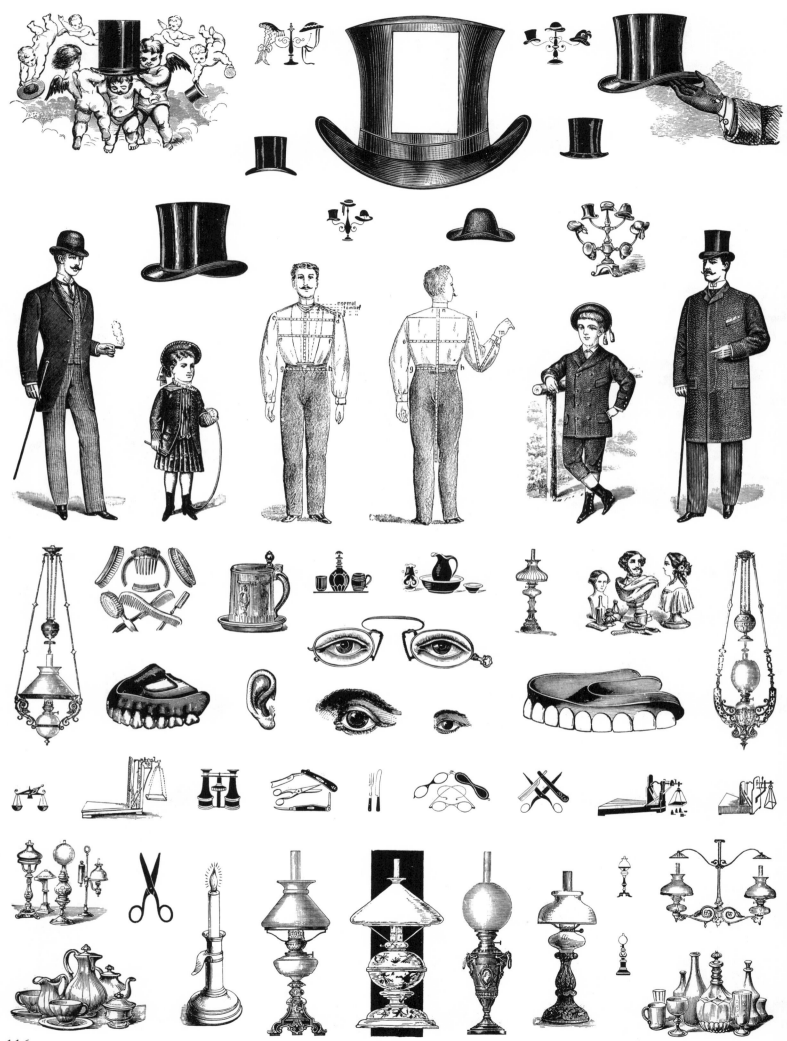

121